House of Ticking Clocks

Mereo Books

2nd Floor, 6-8 Dyer Street, Cirencester, Gloucestershire, GL7 2PF
An imprint of Memoirs Books. www.mereobooks.com
and www.memoirsbooks.co.uk

House of Ticking Clocks
ISBN: 978-1-9191788-7-5

First published in Great Britain in 2025
by Mereo Books, an imprint of Memoirs Books.

Copyright ©2025

Jinny Wilson has asserted her right under the Copyright Designs and
Patents Act 1988 to be identified as the author of this work.

A CIP catalogue record for this book is available from the British Library.
This book is sold subject to the condition that it shall not by way of trade or otherwise be
lent, resold, hired out or otherwise circulated without the publisher's prior consent in any
form of binding or cover, other than that in which it is published and without a similar
condition, including this condition being imposed on the subsequent purchaser.

The address for Memoirs Books can be
found at www.mereobooks.com

Mereo Books Ltd. Reg. No. 12157152

Typeset in 11/19pt Garamond
by Wiltshire Associates.
Printed and bound in Great Britain

House of Ticking Clocks

Memories of Childhood

Jinny Wilson

A collection of fragments, fleeting, kaleidoscopic
snapshots, drawn together
by the thread of childhood memory.

1

I can hear my mother's footsteps on the linoleum, tapping anxiously like her heart beating. I have my Clarks' crêpe-soled sandals on so they make no noise, but my heart is beating fast too, fluttering and uncomfortable in my chest.

The walls of the corridor we're walking down are painted green, pea-soup green, and the floor is polished wood, very shiny and clean. It feels disinfected and the lights, suspended from the ceiling with military precision, have green glass shades; the corridor seems endless, echoey, and the windows to the rooms on each side are too high up for me to see through. Mum holds my hand very tightly, as if she's afraid I'll disappear.

I'm wearing my kilt, Stewart tartan with the funny kilt pin in the corner and done up at the waist with a small leather strap; I have a white blouse and fawn knee-length socks which are a bit itchy, a red cardigan and my blue corduroy windcheater which I really like, a present from my aunt.

The door handles are bright and shiny; it's very quiet and the building seems deserted. I feel as if I'm in the middle of a dream – or a nightmare. The lights are all on, glaring at us. I glance up at Mum, but she is concentrating on something and doesn't glance back at me. She is wearing a soft tweed suit in heathery colours, blue and purple and green which I know she likes, the skirt is straight, the jacket buttoned with horn buttons and she has a small velvet hat on her head so you can't see her wavy hair apart from a few stray wisps sticking out from the side of her hat.

We're nearly at the end of the corridor now and a nurse approaches us. I know she's a nurse because she's wearing a blue and white striped dress, a starched apron and a stiff starched cap.

'Are you supposed to be here?' she barks.

Mum is very tense, almost in tears. She explains, very politely, that we have come to see her daughter, Anthea Kite, who has had her tonsils removed.

The place smells of antiseptic and the nurse looks antiseptic too, like a bottle of TCP, brusque and astringent.

'Follow me,' she snaps.

She pushes the swing door open. We can hear screaming and sobbing. Mum clutches my hand more tightly as we follow the nurse along more green corridors until she stops and points.

'In there.'

We open the door and my sister, who was reading a book, promptly bursts into tears.

Mum sits on the bed and comforts her. We try not to rumple the bedclothes or make the space look untidy. I pull funny faces to make Anthea laugh and she smiles wanly; she looks very pale, white as a sheet as they say.

Mum gets books and comics out of her bag and another nurse comes in with a bowl of jelly and ice cream, which I think looks delicious, and it doesn't seem very fair that I don't have any.

Mum helps Anthea eat a few spoonfuls as the ice cream gradually melts in the bowl and makes a lake around the shards of red jelly and then she helps her start a jigsaw and chats quietly to her while I look out of the window. The sky is grey, grey as the sea and the naval vessels we watch from Sally Port on stormy winter days. Gulls wheel in the wind, splashes of sunlight catching their white wings.

There's a knock on the door. The nurse says it's time for us to go.

Mum hugs my sister. 'We'll be back tomorrow,' she says, 'and then you can come home.'

It's hard leaving her there on her own with just the grey sky to look at.

'She'll enjoy the books,' says Mum.

We catch the bus home. I don't much like being an only child, even for a day.

II

Home is where we start from.

I remember the house where I was born, but only vaguely. There are no photographs of it, the place where I lived for the first five years of my life, from October 1950, so what I describe is like looking through a slightly out-of-focus lens; I can almost grasp it, but then just as the picture seems to settle, it fractures and eludes me again.

It was a semi-detached house in Thurburn Road, North End, Portsmouth. It was probably built in the thirties and had a small front garden with a wooden fence and an American Pillar rose rambling across the palings. The houses down the street were all similar with bay windows, square rooms and linoleum on the floors. Through the green front door is a hallway and at the end of the hall is a sideboard with a clock, ticking away our lives. It's the clocks I remember most, and the puzzle of learning to tell the time.

HOUSE OF TICKING CLOCKS

There were clocks in every room of the house. Everywhere there was ticking. On the mantelpiece in the drawing room was a solid and reliable wooden clock which ticked away the evenings as the room grew darker and the fire flickered and bedtime drew ever nearer.

In my bedroom was my favourite clock – it had been a Christmas present from my granny. It was round and cream coloured, made of metal on a little stand with luminous hands and numbers which glowed in the dark. The face of the clock was a picture of a wood at night; there were toadstools and rabbits and an owl swooped through the moonlit sky while the minutes ticked and tocked with two elves going up and down on a log seesaw. It was on a little table by my bed and was one of my 'best things.' My sister had a clock too, round and cream like mine, but the picture on hers was of a farmyard with cows and a horse and a cockerel and the minutes ticked with a hen and her chicks pecking grain; there was bright blue sky and green fields. I secretly liked her clock better than mine, but I never admitted that.

Granny had the most elaborate clock of all, the winding of which was a ritual. It was a black marble one with little pillars under a portico like a Greek temple. The face in the centre was inlaid with ornate gold patterns, the hands were fine and delicate, curlicued and sharp and the numbers seemed much too grand and decorated for real life. Granny treasured the clock, but it looked to me as though it should be in funeral parlour; it looked like the gateway to Hades.

There was a clock in the kitchen too, a big round one over the back door with Roman numerals, which made telling the time even more confusing.

The clock in the hall was in a brown wooden case. It had a glass door which opened so it could be wound and fancy numbers which were hard to read. The clock was on the sideboard between a very elaborate blue bowl and a large jug; I loved their colours, lapis lazuli blue and pale turquoise with bright orange and yellow splashes. The clock seemed dull and sober against such artistry, but it was solid and reliable and always told the time, and it was there when we got home and measured out our days.

But telling the time was a problem.

I'm tired of playing with Binky by myself and my sister is at school. I go into the kitchen to ask Mum what the time is.

'Well, where is the long hand?' my mother asks patiently.

I scuttle back to look at the clock at the end of the hall.

'The long hand is on the six,' I report as I return to the kitchen.

'And where is the short hand?' Mum asks.

I shuttle back to the hall.

'The short hand is on the twelve.'

Mum is coming out of the kitchen along the dark passageway. She smiles at me, rubbing her hands on her apron.

'And so the time is…?' she prompts gently.

I don't know. It's a huge puzzle, this business of telling the time, but it seems important because things happen at certain times.

'It's half past twelve, lunch will be ready soon, ' says Mum. 'You can play in the garden until I call you in.'

And she goes upstairs to see my rather demanding granny.

I sidle through the kitchen; the table is laid for lunch, blue check tablecloth, knives and forks, cream plates with orange spots, a jug of flowers from the garden, and in the middle of the table the blue pot of salt which we children are never allowed, although all the adults scoop a little pile onto the side of their plates for every meal. My father had a big pile each day. The pot is a beautiful blue, shaped like a wren's nest and it has a tiny ladle. I tiptoe to the table, pick up the ladle and pour the salt into my mouth. But what I had thought would taste delicious is gritty and claggy and hard to swallow; it cakes on my tongue and catches the back of my throat.

I hear Mum coming back to the kitchen. I try to swallow the salt and I want to run outside, but the white stuff sticks to my tonsils and as Mum comes into the kitchen, I'm sick all over the floor. I wouldn't envy people the salt pile again.

Mum, kind and gentle as ever, clears up the mess, gives me a glass of water to sip and calmly goes on getting lunch for everyone.

The kitchen was at the back of the house. Off the hall was the drawing room with wooden mantelpiece and mirror and fireplace and windows looking onto the street. Off the other side of the hall was my Granny's kingdom when she stayed with us. It looked over the garden and always felt green and shady and a bit forbidding, with plant stands for aspidistras and a huge dining room table with a purple velvet cloth hanging down all round it, a good place to hide if you didn't want to be found. Beyond the dining room was the yellow kitchen and scullery and the back door to the garden and the outside world.

As it gets dark the streetlights are lit, still with a lamplighter coming each night with ladder and with lamp; I'm scared to go upstairs by myself, it's so black up there apart from the eerie glow shed by the street lamp onto the landing. The stairs creak and the linoleum floor is cold and unwelcoming; my little bedroom is tiny, just room for a bed – it's above the hall and has a small window overlooking the road. On my bed is Binky, my favourite toy, a strange clockwork puffin that waddles along when you wind it up, and my dog, a small, stuffed, brown terrier who lived for years, becoming more and more hairless with age; there's a bookshelf with a Children's Bible, some Ladybird books of birds and flowers, Jemima Puddleduck, Tom Kitten and Jeremy Fisher and Hymns for Little Children, and a rag rug on the floor by my bed.

My sister's room is much bigger; she has a fireplace and a fire is lit on winter mornings when Jack Frost has drawn icy ferns on the window panes. We dress by the fire, putting on vests, liberty bodices and layers of 'woollies' before tiptoeing along the cold corridor, across the landing and down to the warm kitchen for breakfast.

The best place to play in the house was on the stairs. It's all confused in my mind with the Robert Louis Stevenson poem 'We made a ship upon the stairs….' So I don't know which came first, did we make a ship because of the poem or did we like the poem because we made ships too? We draped sheets and blankets over the banisters, balanced stools precariously on the turn of the risers and sailed away to foreign lands.

We played strange games as children – another favourite was being dentists with Mum's precious needlework box, using all the button hooks and crochet needles for drills and picks on our dolls.

One winter Christmas I was so ill with measles I had to sleep on the sofa in the drawing room by the fire; when I woke up I saw a red dressing gown by my feet, it was a present, but I thought Father Christmas had left his cloak behind……….

We made libraries, piling books up into towers and stamping tickets for the library users and all the toys we had came in and out to choose something to read. We played schools, too; I was always the pupil. My sister was clever and academic, she learnt to read very quickly. Once when she was only five she was reading a newspaper and read a headline to Mum: 'Woman walks into pond'. Then she said, 'What a funny thing to do, why would a woman walk into a pond, it says the water closed over her head?'

Mum somehow had to explain that sad story. Precocious reading is not always a good thing.

But Anthea ate books for breakfast, especially history books, so she directed games of Boudicaa and Hereward the Wake, and we wriggled through marshland and rode in chariots made of cardboard boxes. We watched Alfred the Great burning the cakes and sat with Canute as he tried to hold back the tide. Games lasted for days and days; we dressed up in old sheets for togas or with Mum's silk scarves and velvet jackets for royal personages.

Mostly though, we played in the garden behind the house, down the path beyond the garage. The garden walls were covered with rambling roses, Goldfinch and Seagull, and in the beds the Peace rose, one of Pa's great joys, bred after the war and a precious sign of hope in many suburban plots.

We all loved the garden. Mum loved it for her flowers, roses, lilac, lavender, London Pride, phlox, Michaelmas daisies, chrysanthemums and all the annuals she grew every year like a farmhouse garden. Anthea and I loved it for all the games we played there, imagining we were circus performers walking on flowerpots held taut by string, cycling round and round the lawn on bikes after we had learnt to balance, wobbling, falling, crashing, picking ourselves up again, encouraged patiently by Pa, his spade-like hands always ready to support us and push us off again until we had the confidence to keep pedalling. He calmly played as we learnt to catch balls too, throwing carefully to our cupped hands – delighted if our fingers clutched it, gently remonstrating if it fell at our feet.

'Bad luck Butterfingers, try again,' he would say, and so we did.

In summer, on hot, hot days we ran through the sprinkler on the lawn in our ruched, elasticated swimming costumes, pretending we were swimming the Channel, or we had shops under the trees selling leaves and bunches of flowers…

In winter we made dens in the garage with boxes as boats and we played muffled up in balaclavas, long fawn socks, windcheaters and woollen scarves.

Pa loved the garden because he loved all things growing, and growing all things. He had a vegetable plot behind the garage, potatoes and cabbages in rows, runner beans and lettuces in summer, leeks and parsnips in autumn; he had an allotment too and came back after a day's digging his bike laden with bounty.

III

I'm pulling my toy dog along the hallway, hearing the clocks tick and chime. I'm holding Binky in the other hand because I want to keep them both close. Apart from the clocks it's very quiet – my sister is at school, but it feels strange today because Mum isn't here and my Granny is looking after me. She's very kind, but it's not the same. I know I have to be good and polite and it seems a long time since Mum left. I sit on the bottom stair near the front door thinking that if I wait there long enough, I'll hear Mum's key in the lock. But she's gone to London to see Great Aunt Alice to take Christmas presents to her, she's gone on the train and I don't know where London is, only that it's a long way. I hug my dog a bit closer and wind Binky up to waddle along the hall.

Granny calls me for lunch. I go into the kitchen, and the table is laid just for two people, for her and for me. I sit in my place while she busies about with saucepans. She says she's made parsley sauce to go with 'a little bit of fish' as she calls it, which she likes and I don't. It looks grey and tasteless on my plate but I have to eat it. The parsley sauce helps. We have mashed potato too. Then Granny puts rice pudding in a bowl. Stirred pink with raspberry jam, it's a bit more palatable.

After she's washed up and tidied the kitchen we play Snap. Granny loves playing cards, she lets me win. The afternoon passes, we do some jigsaws and I play with Binky, then Granny bundles me up in my coat and balaclava and mittens and we go to meet my sister from school. We walk home through the darkening street; it's getting colder and the lamplighter will soon come with his ladder to climb up and light the lamps.

When we get to our house it's dark inside and the house is empty; Mum still isn't back.

Granny switches on the lights and 'perks up' the fire in the drawing room. We eat tea, crumpets (Granny likes crumpets) and sandwiches and milk and biscuits; it's a bit dismal. Anthea and I squabble and Granny says we must be good or she will put on her hat and coat and go out and what would we do then? We make some jigsaws, one of a big sailing ship with easy pieces and then one of a jeweller's shop, which is difficult; Granny draws the curtains.

Pa comes in through the kitchen, whistling, jolly as ever, claps his hands when he sees us and twinkles, but he's worried when he hears Mum isn't back. The grown-ups go and talk in the kitchen, then Granny gets us ready for bed. She lets us put on our nightdresses by the fire and brushes our hair and washes our faces. Then Pa takes us up to bed, reads us stories, tucks us up and says goodnight.

But it's so strange without Mum; she's never not been there for us at bedtime before. Pa is jolly but his eyes aren't so twinkly as usual and there isn't the same murmur of evening noises downstairs. I curl up with Binky and Pa says Mum will be home by the morning.

But she isn't.

Pa goes off to work as usual. He's wearing his brown chalk-striped suit, his blue and red striped tie, he takes his brown hat and waves us goodbye, but he looks worried. Granny gets us dressed. She's a bit tetchy and she's cross when we're slow to eat our porridge even when she puts Lyon's Golden Syrup on it. I look at the picture on the tin, of the lion and all the bees and my sister reads 'Out of the strong came forth sweetness.'

'What does that mean?' I ask.

Granny is impatient and tells me not to bother her now. We ask where Mum is and she snaps back, 'Mum is in London.'

'But she was only going for a day,' my sister says.

'Great Aunt Alice isn't well so your mum stayed to look after her.'

The subject is clearly closed. It's a very dark morning. Granny pushes my arms into my tight coat again and we take my sister to school. When we get to the school gate my sister hugs me goodbye and looks sad. She goes through the playground with all the other children; I'm left with Granny.

On the way back I say, 'When's Mum coming home?'

Granny answers crossly, 'I don't know, but I'm doing my best to look after you all.'

Don't know? What does she mean she doesn't know? Grown-ups know everything.

What we didn't know then, but found out later was that a fog, the Great Smog, had descended on London.

Another long, dark day at home feeling discombobulated.

Late that afternoon, after we have met my sister from school and are having tea, there's a knock on the back door. Our kind neighbour Mrs Westbrook is there, scarf over her head, smiling in the dark.

'Come in, come in, it's so good to see you,' says Granny. 'We're all at sixes and sevens here, come in out of the cold.'

Mrs Westbrook gives us each a warm cake she has just baked which brightens up our rather dull plates, then she and Granny go into the hall to talk and we bicker over our tea.

Mrs Westbrook goes back into the dark night and Anthea and I play dentists in the drawing room. We get out Mum's precious sewing case, undo the metal clasp, take out the crochet hooks and start viciously prodding our dolls' teeth.

Pa comes home, less cheerful than usual, and we hear him talking to Granny in the kitchen, then he comes into the drawing room and stands by the fire.

'Mum will be home tomorrow!' he tells us.

She had been caught in the terrible smog in London, a fog which swirled up the River Thames and over the houses, mixing with all the coal smoke and creating the terrifying smog. But she was ok; she had only just been able to make the telephone call to the Westbrooks to tell us she was safe. We didn't have a telephone.

The mood lifts at home. Granny plays endless card games with us and Pa laughs and jokes as he chases us up to bed.

The next day, a Saturday, Pa gardens in the morning and we play and help Granny tidy up. After lunch he takes us to Alexandra Park, me in the pushchair and Anthea running beside us.

It's cold in the park, seagulls wheel overhead mewing. Pa pushes me really fast and then lets go of the pushchair and runs to catch up with it. Trees are leafless and the sky steely grey – my fingers are freezing, the wind chills my cheeks, round and round we go under the trees and it's getting dark as we turn towards home.

As we go up the road, the lights are on in our house.

Pa lifts me out of the pushchair, my sister opens the door. 'Hello?' we call.

Mum calls back, 'Hello, I'm home!'

So life returns to normal.

IV

The year turns. Days grow from the short darkness of midwinter to March gusts and bursts of sunlight. Pa brings bunches of daffodils back from the allotment and crocuses cheer suburban gardens. We get new summer sandals and wear shorts again; the sun is high in the sky and we play under the shade of the apple tree in the garden.

And flags are flying. All along the main roads and down the streets, Union Jacks catch the wind and people plant red, white and blue flowers in their front gardens.

Mum makes new dresses for us for the Coronation; lots of cutting and pinning and stitching and measuring. There is a hazy picture of us standing in front of the Goldfinch rose in the garden, short white socks and polished sandals, dresses with gathered skirts and puffed sleeves. We're holding Union Jacks on sticks. Anthea's hair is tied back with a bow and mine is the usual page boy cut with a short fringe.

But what I remember of the day is not pomp or ceremony.

We cross the road to go the house of Mrs Harris, a neighbour, who has a television. I don't want to go inside, I'd rather stay in our garden, but Mum insists we must go. The road is deserted. We open the wrought iron gate and I catch the scent of privet flowers from the hedge, sweet and slightly sickly; her garden is very tidy, red salvias, blue lobelia and little white alyssum along the borders.

We knock on the front door and hear steps up the hall. The door opens and smart Mrs Harris, hair permed, wearing a silk blouse, tailored skirt and high-heeled shoes, lets us in. It's dark inside. The hall is full of shadows and dark furniture, which we squeeze past, and she opens the door to the drawing room, which is crowded with people. They're all staring at something and the heavy curtains are drawn as if it's dark, but it's daylight outside. It feels as if someone has died.

In the corner of the room is a television, and flickering across it in grainy grey pictures is a coach drawn by horses and a person wearing a crown. Everyone in the room is mesmerised. Some people gasp at the sight of Buckingham Palace and then the Queen standing on the balcony, we're told. We are pushed forward so we can have a good view, but I don't find it very interesting.

The house smells strange, of cooking and fish and fried potatoes and cigarette smoke. A haze of smoke fills the gloom. It feels stifling, no fresh air blowing through the curtains like we have at home; there are Persian cats too weaving between our legs, their long fur brushing our knees, their eyes luminous in the darkness. I want to get out, but I'm squeezed in between unfamiliar neighbours. I stand close to my sister, who looks absorbed by the ceremony and history on the screen.

I look away from the television to try to see Mum and as I turn around a black face smiles down at me, white teeth and full lips and eyes shining in the dark.

I'm terrified.

I wriggle past bottoms and legs and grab Mum's hand; Mrs Harris is passing round glasses of drink, cups of tea, unfamiliar food, but Mum makes our excuses and we escape from the ordeal. We go back across the road to our own gate, the American Pillar rose and the green front door.

Playing in the garden is much more fun than watching the Coronation.

V

Lyndhurst Road Primary School was a brick-built Victorian establishment. It had high windows to let light in without allowing children to look out; it was forbidding, with an entrance for BOYS and a separate door for GIRLS, and we all lined up in the yard before leaving the daylight and going into what might have been thought of as Hades; like Persephone who had eaten the pomegranate seeds, I was condemned to spend most of the daylight hours in winter inside this building. It smelt of a mixture of polish and disinfectant. The wooden floors were highly polished, footsteps echoed past the classrooms and the passageways were lined with pegs where we hung our drab post-war coats.

Class One was the domain of kind Miss Smith; she wore tweed skirts and hand-knitted cardigans with a soft white blouse. She was as comfortable as her clothes. She had grey hair rolled into a bun at the nape of her neck, her face was wrinkled as a winter apple and her eyes pale, distant blue. She made us think learning was a good thing, her teaching, like her shoes, sensible and long lasting.

Around the room, high up by the picture rail was an alphabet frieze in capitals and lower case letters and pictures.

A is for apple

B is for ball C is for cat – or was it candle?

I don't remember D.

Gradually, after daily chanting, we made sense of the code and learnt to read and write. We must have done sums too, but they are hidden too deep to conjure back. We did lots of sticking, making calendars with pictures of flowers or Old Masters, we painted whales and sea creatures and did weaving with scraps of wool.

The highlight of Miss Smith's class for us was the Nature Table and each week we took in things for display, sticky buds which we put in a jam jar and watched unfurl into pale, etiolated leaves, nests of moss and sheep's wool and horse hair which we found in the hedgerows, feathers from magpies and pigeons and jays from the park, frogspawn from the pond, stones from the shore with strange markings, autumn leaves, old man's beard, rose hips, shiny conkers holding such promise and in spring primroses and daffodils and field poppies and grasses in summer.

The playground was like the Wild West to me, boys whirling round, chasing, shouting, punching, girls skipping and loitering, playing hopscotch and tag. I sometimes got caught up in the boys' games and one day when Mum asked what happened at school I said, 'John Cooper punched me on the nose.'

Mum looked worried and amused at the same time.

'So what did you do then?'

'I punched back of course,' I answered.

Mum usually met us at the end of the afternoon when the bell rang, the doors were opened to the outside world and we were free again. Sometimes, if Mum couldn't meet us my sister and I walked home by ourselves and when she had left to go to another school I had to walk home alone, running my fingers along the metal fences, dodging past houses which for some reason seemed frightening, in and out of the shadows of trees.

Today is different. It's October and the sun is shining and as I come out of school Mum is nowhere to be seen, but Pa is waiting for me by the school gate – with his bicycle.

He lifts his hat to Miss Smith and smiles, his bicycle leans by his side and he puts out his spade-like hands to greet me. Then he lifts me onto the saddle of his 'old pushbike' as he calls it and wheels me through the streets. It's like being on the top deck of a bus; I can see over fences and into the neat suburban gardens and front rooms.

It feels like a jolly outing. Pa always makes things feel like that – it's fun, he's home from work early and meeting me from school. But why did he cycle to work with his bicycle clips and pump? He usually drove in his Ford Popular.

October 1956, near my birthday, the Suez Crisis. There is petrol rationing, so the car stays in the garage and Pa makes fun out of necessity and strangely it's the only day I have a clear photographic memory of being met from school.

The world is less sunlit now, November perhaps, grey and cold, it seems dark almost all day and the sky the colour of washing up water swirling down the drain. We shiver as we get dressed and Mum seems less patient than usual this morning. At breakfast she tells us we're not going to school until later today as we have to have injections at a clinic in town. Anthea, who always knows what's going on in the world says, 'Is it because of polio?'

Mum nods. 'It's a horrible illness but this injection will keep you safe. We're going to the clinic today, where they'll give injections to as many children as possible. I'll take you to school afterwards.'

We finish our porridge.

'Will it hurt?'

'It will be a sharp needle in your arm, it will hurt a bit like a pin pricking you, but it will keep you safe.'

We think about this as we eat our toast, then, faces washed, teeth cleaned, coats on, we're ready to go.

Mrs Westbrook, our neighbour, is at our gate as we pass. She chats to Mum and then smiles at us. 'You look like two peas in a pod,' she says.

We're wearing grey school coats and identical socks and shoes. Anthea is not much taller than me, although she is three years older, but she has long plaits, whereas my hair is just short and straight.

The wind is cold as we turn the corner. Fallen leaves and scraps of paper scurry along the pavement, I run my fingers along the garden fences and railings feeling the ridges ripple under my fingers. Mum is walking quickly, it's hard to keep up.

When we reach the clinic there's a long queue outside; people shuffle forward, children in pushchairs, babes in arms, slouching teenagers, every family in Portsmouth seems to be there. I push my hands into my pockets and find a wizened conker. Mum chats to people in the line and we edge towards the doorway.

Inside the hall we're directed to the far end of the room and a nurse brusquely tells my sister to roll up her sleeve as she prepares the syringe. Anthea is brave. Mum looks anxious but my sister doesn't scream or make a fuss and I hover behind Mum, waiting for my turn.

The lights are dim, just a couple of bulbs covered by dirty white shades hanging from wires in the ceiling. The nurse prepares another syringe and tells my sister to roll her sleeve up again. She raises the syringe, gives it a couple of taps to let the liquid settle and then injects my sister a second time.

Mum looks puzzled. Anthea puts her coat on.

'Right, you're both done in this family. Next please!' says the nurse.

Mum pushes me forward.

'This is my second child,' she says.

'But I've done two vaccinations for this family, I've done both children.'

'No,' insists Mum, 'you've given this child two injections.'

The nurse drops the syringe she is holding. The glass shatters and there is silence in the hall. Everyone is looking at us.

A doctor in a white coat approaches us. 'The children are only meant to have one dose each.'

Mum's face is lined with worry. The nurse looks horrified at what she has done. The doctor checks my sister's temperature, her arm, her pulse, her throat...

'Watch her very carefully for the next few days,' the doctor tells Mum. 'Any sign of fever, headache, out of sorts, you must see a doctor immediately.' He enunciates the word slowly and clearly as if to put great emphasis on it.

People start muttering and murmuring behind us; I can see other mothers glancing sympathetically at Mum, sorry for her trouble but relieved their own child is safe. The queue shuffles forward. Another nurse comes over to us. Whilst Mum can't take her eyes off Anthea, the nurse rolls up my sleeve.

'I'm just going to give you a quick jab,' she says. 'Only the one, mind. Be brave to help your mum and sister. What's your name?'

I offer my arm, a lamb to the slaughter. The nurse jabs the needle in quickly, then, putting the syringe down, she helps me to put on my coat. The long line of families edges forward into the hall, unaware of our drama, like the ploughboys in the painting of the Fall of Icarus.

Anthea looks all right. She hasn't grown extra ears or horns, she looks a bit white but she can still walk and talk. The nurse leads us to a small room away from the crowds. She gives Mum a cup of tea and squash and biscuits for us. A doctor comes in; he appears very serious. He talks quietly to Mum while the nurse asks Anthea and me about school and where we live, trying to distract us from the adult conversation.

After a few minutes, we are ushered out of the hall and Mum hurries us home.

'No school today,' she says. 'We'll have school at home instead.'

The clock in the hall ticks away the day. Mum doesn't let us out of her sight even for a second. She takes Anthea's temperature regularly, sticks the glass thermometer under her tongue, shakes it professionally, looks at the thin red line and is relieved.

She gives us Ribena to drink, and Lucozade; she makes rock cakes with us, makes shops out of kitchen packets, we have a till with real money for change, we write shopping lists and turn the drawing room into a dolls' hospital where we take temperatures, feel pulses, give medicine and vaccinations and write prescriptions.

'But you only need one jab,' my sister insists to all the toys.

No school the next day either; we make ships on the stairs, still the waves with Canute, cut pictures from cards for scrapbooks and do jigsaws.

By the third day we're allowed to go to the Library in town, a tall, imposing building, to change our books; temperatures are only taken at breakfast and bed time. By the weekend things are almost normal; the terrible fate of catching polio by being vaccinated twice has been avoided. We can all breathe again.

The year rolls on.

VI

'Come, the pear tree is in blossom.'

A card arrived at home which Mum reads to us, she seemed pleased to get it, and now we are on our way to Miss Flowers' house in Portsmouth.

It's early April and the sun is shining through the dusty windows of the trolley bus. On the pavement people are scurrying past, women with hats and baskets, delivery boys on bicycles, newspaper sellers call 'the latest' from their stands on street corners, an old man with one leg and crutches leans against the library building. He's often there when we go past, but today the sun brightens the greyness and shadows stretch between buildings, and it all unfolds before us like a page from Dickens.

We are wearing the Sunday dresses which Mum made for us; mine is pale blue with a dark blue sash and Anthea's is green. Our hair is brushed neatly, Anthea's in long plaits and mine with a too-short fringe. Socks are pulled up and shoes, as always, polished by Pa.

The itchy seats on the bus scratch the backs of our legs, but at last Mum pulls the rope which dings the bell, the bus stops, we clamber downstairs and alight outside a big old house with iron railings and gates and steps up to the front door.

Mum holds my hand and reminds us to be polite and the door is opened by a maid wearing a black dress, a small white apron and a white, frilly cap. She looks rather washed out, like a flat balloon. We are led down a black and white tiled hall with a chandelier glinting above us into the drawing room where Miss Flowers is waiting. The room has long windows overlooking the garden and is filled with furniture, ornate clocks and delicate china figurines.

Miss Flowers was one of the original Girton girls at Cambridge who Mum had met when she attended the Workers Educational Association Lectures at the Library. Miss Flowers gave the lectures and she had befriended Mum and would send cards, imperiously, at different times of the year.

'Come, the holly berries are aglow in the garden.'

'The quinces are ripe, come for tea.'

'Visit me while the roses are in bloom.'

She is a large person, and her presence fills the room. She is dressed in long, glamorous silky clothes, she has rows of pearls round her neck and her white hair is swept back in an elegant bun.

'My dears, I'm glad you've come, let us go into the garden and admire the pear tree.'

She leads the way through the French windows and onto the lawn. The garden is huge, surrounded by walls and laurel hedges, there is a shrubbery, dark and uninviting, formal rose beds and herbaceous borders, a lawn where a cedar of Lebanon casts shade, a vegetable garden like a display of lead soldiers with every plant in line, greenhouses, an orchard and in the centre of it all the pear tree, colossal and magnificent, towers above us, flowers tumbling from the branches like froth on a pail of milk.

Anthea and I are left to play on the lawn while Miss Flowers shows Mum all her prize plants. We run in and out of the shrubbery like sparrows, collect petals scattered on the grass and wander in the warmth of the vegetable garden. It's another world.

Then Miss Flowers claps her hands, and we go to find the adults and go inside for tea.

The dining room has lace curtains over the windows and a lace cloth covers the table. The maid lifts silver covers from all the plates.

'Now my dears, sandwiches first, then bread and butter and then you may have cake.'

The maid offers us cucumber sandwiches, the bread and cucumber sliced so thinly that they are almost transparent. We drink milk from fine bone china cups and Miss Flowers pours tea from silver teapots into flower patterned cups.

'China or Darjeeling?' she enquires.

We watch mesmerised as she puts a slice of lemon into her teacup. Whoever heard of lemon in tea?

Then we have slices of bread and butter which we spread with honey from a little pot shaped like a beehive.

'Honey from my bees,' intones Miss Flowers.

Then there is seed cake, gritty and disgusting, but after that Victoria sponge thick with strawberry jam and cream, and finally a plate of chocolate biscuits.

At last tea is finished.

'Now my dears, you may play in the garden until your Papa comes.'

We feel as though we are in a Victorian novel, that somewhere upstairs we will hear the sound of a child crying or a ghost wafting along the gravel paths of the shrubbery.

We go out and play hide and seek, make collections of fallen petals on leaf plates and find corners of warmth in patches of sunlight among the vegetables.

And there is Pa, striding across the lawn, and his spade-like hands scoop us up and whirl us round on the grass. He chases us across the garden as the shadows lengthen, then we brush ourselves down as we go back into the formidable drawing room. Miss Flowers gives us each a book, ones from her childhood which she thinks we will like. We thank her, say goodbye and the maid opens the door and we run down the steps, through the iron gate and we sit all anyhow, giggling with relief in the back of Pa's car as he drives us home.

VII

Sometimes, on Saturday afternoons in winter or when Pa came home from work on summer evenings, we'd have an expedition to the Camber, the harbour in Old Portsmouth. We walked along the docks and wharves where towering cargo ships were tied up. Sometimes we saw them unloading crates of fruit, pallets swinging precariously from cranes and landing with amazing accuracy on the stack on the quay. We saw boxes of oranges, cauliflowers, potatoes, and what Pa loved most to see, consignments of bananas swaying out from the holds; he always dreamed of going on a banana boat to the West Indies and seeing the world unfold beyond the sea.

Sometimes we saw the great ships coming in to dock, engines grinding, water churning round the bows, the captain on the bridge shouting commands, tugboats with tyres all along their gunwales manoeuvring the huge behemoths into place and the dockers on the side ready to catch the ropes which drew steel hawsers round capstans until the maelstrom settled, the water stilled, the engines were silent and voyages ended.

There were naval ships in the harbour too, painted battleship grey and as orderly and smart as a sailor on parade, ropes neatly coiled, paintwork spotless, metal gleaming and decks swabbed.

I was fascinated by the iridescence of petrol spilled on puddles on the quays and in the water, swirling and creating endless patterns of colour like a kaleidoscope or the sheen on pigeon's feathers; fascinated by sailors from different countries, foreign, exotic, speaking odd, guttural words, and the cold, metallic feel of the capstans and their strange shapes like Henry Moore sculptures, the smell of the sea and salt and the sound of gulls mewing and bickering overhead.

We stayed until it grew dark and the lights came on in ships around the harbour, all reflected in the water like stars.

VIII

After the war, maybe when land was cheap, Pa bought a plot on the edge of Bedhampton, a village in the country along the coast from Portsmouth, out towards the small market town of Havant. In the oldest part of the village, near the marshes, was St Thomas' Church; in the centre were shops, a chemist, grocer and wine merchant, a village school and Bedhampton Halt, where trains stopped en route from Portsmouth Harbour to London Waterloo.

In 1955 he planned a home and had it built in Hulbert Road, which was then a country lane. It was a solid brick-built house with an oak front door, hardwood floors, a cloakroom for coats, a drawing room overlooking the long front garden, dining room across the back of the house, kitchen, scullery and coal stores. Mum chose lovely wallpapers for the bedrooms; one had wildflowers painted on it, poppies, cornflowers and buttercups, and another was cow parsley and grasses against a pale green background. There was a modern bathroom and a big airy landing. My bedroom looked across the back garden to the orchard and woods and fields.

I remember the sickly sweet scent of privet from the overgrown hedges bordering the garden, and the septic tank which Pa said was full of 'jungle juice', which he used to water the vegetables. Mum grew lots of flowers scattered from seed packets, cornflowers, larkspur, mignonette, sweet Williams, marigolds; she always had a jug of flowers on the table or in the fireplace. In spring pussy willow glinted silver in the hedge and in summer mare's tails and bindweed grew freely in the heavy clay soil. Days and days were spent playing in different parts of the garden, climbing ash trees and apple trees; in autumn we had bonfires; in winter we built snowmen and tobogganed on a silver sledge until our mittens were frozen and fingers and feet so cold we almost cried; in spring we found frogspawn in the ditches and on summer days we made tents on the lawn from washing lines and sheets.

The clocks were there too, the kitchen clock over the back door, the brown wooden clock lived in the dining room and our gnomes and chickens ticked away the hours in our bedrooms and I gradually made sense of the hands and numbers.

IX

It's like landing in another country, this first day at another school. A child of Low Anglican parents in a world of nuns and Roman Catholicism.

Mother van Heems, Head of the Lower School, greets us and shows me where to put my coat and beret with its special blue silk tassel, then leads me to Transition.

I am in Miss Ball's class; she is old and grey and wrinkled and she sits down a lot. We gather in the classroom, in itchy new school uniform, Miss Ball calls the register in a quavery voice, then we walk in silence down the corridor to The Grotto, (what is a grotto, I wonder?) and we stand in rows with the rest of the school. Candles flicker on the altar and the statue of 'Our Lady', white as marble, cold as stone, but with a sweetly smiling face, holds out her hands to us. There are flowers on the altar, or greenery, always something to honour 'Our Lady' (as I must learn to call Mary, the mother of Jesus); then the singing starts:

'Soul of my Saviour, sanctified for me.' Old Sister Ursula shuffles in the back, leaning on a stick, her face so lined from life you can hardly distinguish her eyes and mouth among the contours, her back so bent she can barely stand, but still she comes. Sister Patricia, austere, pale faced, upright, sings above all the rest of the nuns.

The hymn ends. Everyone mumbles some prayers, which are like a foreign language. I'm screwing my eyes together, pretending they are closed and I'm praying. But the next bit of Catholic ritual defeats me. I don't know how to do it. I don't know how to make the sign of the cross. Everyone else does it like a frog swims, but for me it seems a magical trick I will never fathom. Where do I start? At the top, the bottom, left, right, which hand should I use?

I squint sideways, trying to see the pattern the others are making, and just as I do this Mother van Heems intones, 'Amen.' Everyone opens their eyes wide. I feel they are all looking at me because I am the only one not to be initiated, not to know the ritual.

'The black babies are all climbing the steps to heaven, thanks to your generosity.' The voice of Mother van Heems draws everyone back to look at her. 'And today five more children in far-away parts of the world will achieve salvation and education. Now you may go, children.'

We file back to our classrooms, and as we go towards the crocheting comfort of Miss Ball a hand gently touches my shoulder.

'My child, a moment of your time.'

I look into the kindly face of the Dutch nun, who could have poured milk in a painting by Vermeer. I stand still. I have been found out. Now I will be handed over to the devil and all his works because I don't know how to make the sign of the cross.

'I'm sorry,' I stutter, 'I just don't know how to…'

'My child, I will show you the way.'

And with firm, work-worn, gentle hands she guides me through the ritual. I promise to practise, and that night I do it at home over and over again in front of the mirror at the foot of the stairs until I have mastered the mystery.

Reading was easy. It was the religious mysteries I found so hard to learn and understand.

Back in the classroom, Miss Ball, still sitting down and by now doing her knitting, gives me a Ladybird book.

Janet and John are at home.

Janet and John are in the garden.

Janet and John have a dog. The dog is called Pat.

I am on my way. The doors are being unlocked, I am learning to read, one of the things I'll love best for the rest of my life.

I get used to the mysteries, the language and arcane rituals, I get used to Miss Ball nodding in her chair while we do arts and crafts with Mother Zeoul, an ancient crone who brings bags full of cardboard tubes and pots of glue and raffia and shows us how to make mats and calendars and napkin rings and other useless, treasured objects. I trot along to the Grotto almost like a good Catholic child and am confident enough to sneak to the Chapel with a friend at playtime.

I like the Chapel at the Convent, although it's very different from the parish church of St Thomas beside the stream at home. This Catholic chapel is among the tunnel of buildings by the Convent House across the playground from school. We go there for services on 'special days' of obligation with everyone else and then it's like going to a lesson.

Sometimes at breaktime we creep in by ourselves. Then it's dark and the candle is burning low to show the sacrament is present; it feels as though someone is watching us. We creak open the door, dip our fingers in the holy water stoup, make the sign of the cross (it's like a lucky charm), and there she is again, The Virgin Mary staring down at us – we genuflect and hurry past. We've been set a dare, to visit all the stations of the cross in less time than it takes to play a game of jacks. The Chapel smells of incense, spicy and exotic, but there is also a lingering smell of boiling cabbage (the chapel is next to the kitchens) and the homely scent of beeswax polish.

The wooden pews gleam, a shaft of sunlight falls through the high windows. It is peaceful but I'm always on my guard; I can never get over the feeling that I shouldn't be here, I don't have a passport to this country, I don't understand about Penance and Extreme Unction, but I do learn my catechism and for ever afterward I feel the twitch upon the thread, what might have been.

Twelve Stations completed, we scuttle out into the sunlight and I can breathe freely again.

We play in the yard between the Convent House and straggle of school buildings. Sometimes, especially in summer, we play in the sandpit in the garden of St Joseph's cottage, but I think that's only on special occasions, holy days maybe.

One day, when I'd been elevated to the Juniors, beyond kind Miss Ball's class, we have a lesson about The

Eclipse, another new word to me. Is this part of religion too? I store it up in my memory. Our teacher is Miss Kelly, Irish with red hair and green eyes; I don't like her much and I don't think she likes me. I am not Irish, I am not Catholic, I ask questions which she doesn't answer, I am an annoyance. This particular morning she tells us, 'You'll see a dark cloud coming and darkness will cover the whole earth.'

I put my hand up politely.

'But why will it be dark? It's daytime, it doesn't get dark till bedtime, so why will it be dark?'

She waves my question away and tells us all to wash our hands and go and have lunch.

Now I'm sitting in the sandpit in St Joseph's Cottage garden, sand is trickling through my fingers and the day is warm. I make imprints in the sand with my hands, splay my fingers open and press them down. Other children are playing on the grass, doing handstands, teasing, chasing, falling, bullying, squabbling, laughing. Playtime feels longer than usual, a sense of waiting, of something about to happen, and although I've not been aware of birds singing, I realise that all seems quiet and hushed and as I sit in the sand, grains rubbing against my skin and inside my socks, I'm aware that what we've been waiting for is coming.

We're in summer dresses, blue and white gingham, white collars and buttons, pockets for handkerchiefs, white socks, Sunray sandals, the leather still stiff and buckles hard to master; the boys have blue Aertex shirts and grey shorts and they're driving trucks and cars through the sand and making engine noises that I'm envious of. Sand keeps trickling through my fingers, the silence deepens and the sky darkens, darker and darker in the middle of the day, darker than storm clouds, until the whole sky is veiled like night.

We stop. We are still and silent.

We look up from our handstands and our skipping and scrabbling in sand and we are still. Darkness covers the sun. There is no light.

The eclipse.

We hold our breath; it's like the Second Coming we are told so much about at our Convent school. And then it's gone. The darkness passes, the sun shines, sand trickles through my fingers. We go back to class.

At the end of each Lent Term we were given a special treat. Instead of lessons between break time and lunch we crocodile to the Convent House, the holy of holies. It is an honour, a privilege, to enter the old beeswax smelling dining room. We sit on the polished floor, chattering sparrows among the nun-like rooks; blinds are drawn over the long sash windows and the room is in darkness, which induces silence among us.

We turn from each other to stare at the bare white wall. It is as if a miracle is about to happen, water into wine, the blind man given sight.

There is a whirring sound, as of a swarm of bees, portrayed in the wall we see scene after scene of the Life and Passion of Our Lord building up through the calling of the disciples, the miracles of the stilling of the storm and walking on water to that fateful, chilling moment when Judas Iscariot kissed the cheek of Jesus to betray him to the Roman soldiers.

The full weight of sin.

We file out in silence and then, free as birds, we run and betray each other in the playground.

On saints' days in autumn, spring and summer the treat was unforgettable.

St Francis	4th October
St Luke	18th October
St Mark	21st April
St John the Baptist	24th June
St Swithun	15th July

We knew them all, red-letter days in the Missal and red-letter days for us too. We had Chapel at the beginning of the day, all shuffling into the stained-glass window light, candles flickering, the gold crucifix gleaming. We dipped our fingers into the holy water stoup, crossed ourselves, knelt and rattled off our prayers, sang saintly hymns, excitement bubbling inside us. If this was what saints and religion were about they were a good thing, because after Chapel, instead of being pent up in classrooms, we ran through the formal gardens to the fields and woods surrounding the Convent buildings. After tracking down an overgrown path, dodging under brambles and skirting ponds, we reached a clearing with a circle of tree stumps that was base camp for the day. There sat Sister Ursula with her knitting and Sister Patricia with her ashen face, and after the usual talk from Mother van Heems about how good Catholic children should behave we were free to explore the woods, make dams and dens, balance on logs, ambush and attack each other, free to play all day.

When we heard the Angelus bell ringing we descended from all directions to sit in the stump circle, say Grace and eat our lunch. This was always the same. We had cheese sandwiches wrapped in greaseproof paper, a Penguin biscuit and an apple each in our own brown paper bag.

Lunch finished, Grace said again, we continued our games all the long afternoon until the bell called us back to the nuns, who led us back through the gardens to our classrooms, where we collected our belongings to catch the bus home.

I thought God was a combination of good luck and good judgement, but being Catholic and Irish definitely helped. All saints' days were special, but 17th March was more special than most. The day of the Great Netball Match. Every year, for weeks before the event, the older girls had to offer evidence of being Irish or English, because only the truly Irish could play for the Irish Netball team. Competition was fierce.

'My great-great granny's mother was Irish so I must be Irish too…'

'My uncle's mother's brother's parrot was Irish so I'm sure…'

With my fair plaits, blue eyes, pink cheeks and stocky build I could be nothing but Anglo Saxon English. The Irish were always taller, cleverer, more athletic, with red or dark hair, green or brown eyes and had confidence in their natural superiority; they arrived on St Patrick's Day with shamrocks pinned to their blazers and they always, always won the match. The Irish team wore green bibs over their netball kit, the English wore red and the teams ran down to the asphalt court, where if you fell over your knees were grazed to ribbons. Nuns trooped down from the kitchens and daily tasks like a parliament of rooks, and all children not selected for teams gathered round the court.

Mother van Heems blew the whistle and play began. Goals piled into the net for the Irish, whose goal shooter was the size of an Irish giant and clearly had the blessings of all the Irish saints. The result was always about 17-2 against England. Perhaps it wasn't just that being Irish and Catholic gave you the advantage – maybe God really was on their side.

After the match was Gauntlett's tea in the refectory; egg sandwiches, cheese sandwiches, currant buns, iced buns, sponge cake with red jam, pink wafer biscuits and chocolate fingers...

Gauntlett's dairy delivered lunches to the Convent each day, a van with canisters of stew, mashed potato, liver and bacon, steak and kidney pie, spam and salad in summer, fish pie on Fridays and lots of overcooked cabbage.

We ate in the refectory, a converted cow shed, rough built and whitewashed, filled with trestle tables, and when we were bidden we filed to where the nuns stood behind steaming cauldrons like the witches from Macbeth; they dolloped food onto our plates, a splatter of stew, clump of mashed potato, a ladle of wet cabbage, all topped with greasy gravy. We sat down and bowed our heads for Grace before we could eat.

Eating lunch was often an ordeal, stew more gristle than meat, cabbage like slimy seaweed, but only if your plate was clean were we allowed pudding. One day Paul Johnson, a small, scrawny boy, could not swallow the potato, gravy and gristle congealing on his plate, and tears ran down his face as he tried to clear the mountain of food. The eagle eyes of the nuns seemed always to be on us but when Sister Patricia, the termagant, was distracted for a second, Paul took his handkerchief from his pocket and scooped the gravy, potatoes, stew and cabbage into the hanky, folded it up and stuffed it in his blazer. It bulged. It oozed. But when Sister Patricia returned her gaze towards him, she beamed.

'There you are now, that will make a man of you! Go along and fetch your pudding.'

Paul went.

Sometimes we had creamy rice pudding with red jam, sometimes chocolate cake and pink blancmange, apple crumble, jam roly-poly, spotted dick, stewed prunes, and sometimes in the summer blackcurrants and Gauntlett's vanilla ice cream.

After we told Mum about Paul and the handkerchief Mum gave us packed lunches; we missed the ice cream, but not the gristle and gravy.

Packed lunches were eaten in the Kindergarten with kind Mother Zeoul, her face as wrinkled as a turtle's neck, and as we munched our ham sandwiches, home-made cake and apples she spent the time stamping out metal toothpaste tubes and flattening foil sweet papers to send to a needy Catholic children's home – who knows what they did with them, but we collected them faithfully for her and she blessed us.

In winter, when it was very cold, we crowded round the stove in the 'Babies' classroom to drink warm milk from little glass bottles. I hated the milk, the claggy feel as I swallowed it and the cloudy taste, which was even worse when it was warm. It took me ages to drink and the paper straw we sipped through grew soggy. One morning, when my straw had almost dissolved, Mother van Heems came in and tapped me on the shoulder.

'Follow me, my child,' she murmured.

I followed.

All eyes were on me, everyone probably relieved that the tap on the shoulder had not been for them. I put my half-full bottle back in the crate and scuttled in the wake of her black habit.

When we reached the empty corridor, she turned to me. 'Your sister has had an accident, you need to come and comfort her.'

She led me to her study. My sister was sitting on a chair, blood running down from her chin, trickling over a wad of bandage and onto her fingers and culottes. She looked very scared. Sister Patricia was administering care in her usual efficient manner, it was like being cared for by an alabaster statue.

Mother van Heems directed me to a stool which she had placed beside Anthea's chair, but far from comforting her I burst into tears and sobbed and sobbed, the comforter becoming the one who needed comfort.

They took the bandage away from Anthea's chin, revealing a deep gash which they had painted with vile looking yellow liquid and this, mingled with blood, made everything a messy orange colour. The nuns busied round clearing up the mess, cleaning grazed knees and hands; teasing grit from the cuts was a painful process. I gradually stopped crying. Anthea was very brave and then Mum appeared to take her home. I had to return to Miss Ball's class and do arithmetic and reading and make raffia mats until home time. I worried all day about going home without my sister; I had never done that before, she was always there to show me the way.

But I managed. I caught the bus to Waterlooville, paid my twopenny fare, then crossed the road and caught the 31 bus (fourpenny fare) to Havant and Chichester, which dropped us off near our house in Bedhampton. I ran along the road, climbed the five-bar gate and raced down the drive to the front door. Mum was there, and Anthea with a big bandage all over her chin.

Days passed, summer to winter, and we were usually alone at the bus stop near our house waiting for the 31 bus to take us to school. But suddenly they appeared one morning, Barbara and her mother Mrs Woroncow – it was officially pronounced Voronsoff, but once we had seen it written down on her exercise books and name tapes, we pronounced it the way it was spelt.

The mother was large and seemed old for a mum. She was very sturdy and stolid in an East European way, a scarf over her head, boots on her feet, and she always walked slowly and purposefully. Barbara was stolid too, rather pasty or even pastry faced, her hair brushed and pulled back into complicated hairstyles, her socks pulled up, her tie straight and her homework finished.

Where had they come from?

How could people just *appear* in a village, landing like something from Outer Space or Outer Mongolia? I think we weren't very kind to Barbara. She seemed dull and plodding, but she was a good Catholic, so she had more claim to going to the Convent than we did. She wandered round the playground at school looking lost with her broken accent and sad, distant eyes, she didn't fit easily into wild games of tag or Horses or Hide and Seek that we played at break times.

What place had been her home? Where was she dreaming of or remembering?

Mum was always kind to everyone, especially outcasts and refugees, so she invited the Woroncows to tea. The mothers sat and chatted politely with cups of tea and cake, but once we had finished our eggs on toast and cake and biscuits, we had to entertain Barbara. She didn't know how to play any of our games, or how to be imaginative, she didn't like the train set or our camps round the house and garden, she couldn't ride a bike or leapfrog on the grass or climb trees. She would rather sit inside like a little grown up, knitting or sewing. Perhaps it was partly the language, or culture, or being the child of elderly parents. It must have been so strange for her, this English existence.

We had to go back to tea at the Woroncow house, but at least there were two of us. We had to eat Polish meatballs and chewy bread and pastries that were pale and leaden looking and then we played polite 'sitting down' games and her mother tried to teach us to crochet. It was a great relief when Mum came to take us home.

But suddenly, just as suddenly as the Woroncows had appeared in the village, they were gone and we were alone at the bus stop again. We thought her father was a spy and they had to keep moving on; he was a very undistinguished looking man on the few occasions we saw him, or maybe he was in the Polish Mafia and needed to disappear into an English village for a while, or worked for the KGB and was sending them information about all our lives.

Like migrant birds, but with much less grace, they flew in, were with us for a while and then flew on, leaving no trace.

We went on waiting at the bus stop, learning our tables, playing our imaginary games and growing...

Mum, Anthea and me, 1951

Pa and us in the garden in Portsmouth, 1951

Coronation, 1953

Beadon Farm, Somerset

JINNY WILSON

Down to the duckpond

In the apple orchard

Pa by the farm door at Beadon

Autumn on the farm

Collecting cider apples

Newton Ferrars, an expedition from White Oxen

On the granary steps, White Oxen

X

On Saturday afternoons in winter we went to the library, a new, modern building with big windows and low ceilings, a beacon of hope in the Macmillan era of education for all. We return our books, collect our tickets and the search begins, pony books, history books, adventures, travel, classics, the choice is endless. On the way home we choose a quarter of sweets from the shop where Pa gets his tobacco, rainbow drops for me, aniseed balls for Anthea, Bournville chocolate in gold foil and red paper for Mum, and when we get home the fire is lit, crumpets toasted and the evening stretches out with the books to take us to other worlds than these. One of the books we read was *Treasure Island*.

We went to Guides on Thursday evenings, but sometimes we had meetings on Saturday afternoons at the church hall in the middle of the village, a mile or so from home. We usually walked there and back in daylight but once the meeting had gone on longer than expected.

It is dusk when we leave the hall. We shout 'Goodbye!' to everyone and cross the road.

By the time we have walked through the new estate, brightly lit and friendly, houses close to the path with small neat gardens to our lane, it is getting dark. Here the houses have long gardens, the only lights we can see are faint and far away, lamp posts are set far apart and the circle of light they shed is small and dim.

A few cars pass us; we walk on, each pretending to be unconcerned.

I hear a tapping behind us. Anthea hears it too and we quicken our pace - we don't look behind. The hairs on the back of my neck prickle, my hands are sweaty and my heart beats faster. It's like Blind Pew in *Treasure Island*, tapping, tapping, tapping his way along the road. We don't speak, my sister and I, both instinctively thinking that 'it', whatever was making the tapping, would hear us. Anthea sidles up to me and whispers that we must run.

I glance at her, she nods, we start off but I run out of breath, we falter and she slows down, realising I can't keep up with her. Branches stretch out across the lane, long fingers to clutch our hair. A cat crosses our path, unconcerned, tail high in the air, tap, tap, tap……..

Anthea whispers we must do Scouts' Pace, run from lamp post to the next and then walk to the next pale circle of light. We try it, we cover the distance more quickly and feel a bit less scared until we reach the part of the lane with no houses, no lights, just trees and darkness.

Tap, tap, tap…

Should we take the other lane, which makes it further to home but at least there are a few houses, or should we go on the main lane which runs past the spooky spinney?

Blind Pew is coming for us. There is no escape.

We take the deserted, lightless lane and run, run and stagger and run again until we see the lights of home. We race down the drive, swing the gate shut behind us and fall in through the door.

XI

He's called Snowy and I've wanted him for ages. I've badgered Mum endlessly about wanting a pet of my own; everyone in books has at least one pet, dogs or cats or ponies. We have a dog called Pippin, a wire-haired fox terrier, and I love rubbing my nose in her soft sandy ears, but she's not mine. I want a pet of my own.

One day a hutch arrives from a friend – a big wooden hutch with a dark sleeping area and a 'day area' with a wired front section like French windows. We put the hutch on a wooden table by the house and I fill it with straw from a bale in the garden which Pa has for the strawberries.

I imagine a sweet, chestnut brown and dark brown rosetted guinea pig with bright, soft black eyes like sloes, a guinea pig like my friend Sarah from school has, that you can play with on the grass and tell secrets to and dress in dolls' clothes and have animal sports days with, and I'll love it and look after it and feel its veiny scratchy feet on my hands.

Then Snowy arrives.

I don't know where he came from. I didn't think pets could be such a disappointment. He's white, and his fur, instead of being soft and curly, is white and coarse and stiff and he has long, white whiskers and sharp teeth and he looks like a rat. He has red eyes.

He spends all his time in the dark cupboard part of his hutch and only comes out for food, bits of limp cabbage, ends of cucumber and disgusting guinea pig mix. I put him on the grass and try to make friends with him; he bites me and then when I find clover and dandelions for him he runs away to hide in the vegetables. I make him a run on the lawn, edged with stones, covered with chicken wire, lots of space for a guinea pig to prosper.

I build obstacle courses for him with tunnels and stones, but he stares at me from his red eyes and freezes on the grass, refusing to move.

I put him in the dolls' pram and wheel him round the garden, but he wriggles to get out and almost jumps over the side; when I grab him he bites me again, harder this time. It draws blood and his teeth marks are on my hand.

I feed him most days. I give him fresh water and

carrots, but I don't like him. So the civil war continues. We have endless skirmishes, playing, biting, gnawing, escaping, being imprisoned again. Autumn comes and he retreats to his hutch and mostly to the sleeping quarters. I give him more straw as it gets colder and extra carrots. He never smiles.

One winter morning it's cold and raw, it's been snowing and the garden is white. I put on my boots and stomp outside, feeling cross that I have to feed something I don't even like and it's not fair before I go to school and have all my homework to pack in my bag.

I know I didn't clean out his cage last week, even though I told Mum I'd done it. The straw is a bit smelly and not really deep enough for him. My fingers are freezing against the metal latch. He's not snuffling up for his food with his nasty great teeth and ugly red eyes accusing me.

He must be in the cupboard bit. I open the other door; he's hunched up in the corner.

I throw his food in and poke him with a stick to wake him. He doesn't move.

He lies on his side, his skittery feet bent funnily. His eyes are wide open, unblinking. I push my fingers towards him; his body is cold, he doesn't flinch. I lift him out of the straw. His body feels strange and odd and I realise he is lifeless, a dead weight in my hands.

I walk guiltily to the kitchen. Mum is hurrying me for school. I show her what has happened.

'We'll put him in a shoebox,' she says calmly, 'and we'll bury him later. I don't think guinea pigs like such cold weather. Come and put on your scarf and get your satchel. It's all right, I'll take care of Snowy.'

I do what I'm told and cross the road to catch the bus to the Convent.

All that day I feel the Virgin Mary's eyes following me, knowing it was my fault. I didn't clean out the hutch properly. It was my fault Snowy died because I didn't really like him. At break time Sarah and I do the Stations Of the Cross in chapel as penance.

After school Mum helps me bury him in the orchard under the snowy earth. We make some twigs into a cross to put on his grave.

We have jacket potatoes and poached eggs for tea. It's warm and cosy inside.

Pa burns the hutch on the bonfire. Grass grows over the grave.

The year rolls on…

XII

It's March, catkins blowing in the hedges and the garden wakening, earth brown and dry as tobacco dust. We spend the morning mooching about the orchard, imagining we're milking cows, feeding our ponies, collecting eggs from chickens. Now we've made a plan to go to the woods.

The woods are close to home, they'd been coppiced long ago but are now overgrown and brambled. Hazel buds are breaking, creased, folded leaves like pleated silk skirts, chestnuts with fat sticky buds tempting to touch, great oak trees with gnarled, twisted branches and scrubby bushes of hawthorn. Among the trees are some old tyres and rusting tin cans which lend a slight menace to the shadows, but celandines glow in the sun, by the pond marsh marigolds blaze and among the moss primroses in rosettes of crinkled leaves, bees hanging warm air, soft silver rabbit ears on the willow branches and blackbirds chinking, insects whirring.

After lunch we meet the boys next door by our gate. There's Ian, who's a bit older than my sister, and Neil, who's a bit older than me; they're tall and gangly. Their dad's a doctor and drives fast cars.

We take jam jars with string round the necks to carry them easily and go off up the lane. The woods aren't far, but when we get there, although it's a bright March day and sunny in the fields, they are filled with long shadows.

The tracks are muddy and among the overgrown saplings and brambles we see bits of old bicycles, tangles of wire, car tyres, an old saucepan. We squelch across the stream and make a base by a hollow oak tree. The boys get out catapults and show off their skills, they try to teach us how to use them, but I'm not much good at it so the idea palls; they suggest playing Hide and Seek and Ian, the oldest, is 'it' and we scatter as he counts. I trip over brambles and almost fall in to a nettle patch.

'Coming, ready or not!' echoes faintly through the trees.

I'm deep in the wood now. I crouch down behind a thick holly tree, its leaves sharp and glossy. There's a sound of twigs snapping, pigeons cooing, a chiffchaff calling. The moss is damp and cold where I'm hiding, I have a hole in my boots and my feet are wet from the stream. No one comes.

I rub my hand on the rough bark of the tree, a squirrel skitters across branches. I have that funny feeling in my throat like walking over shingle, it's unnerving.

More twigs snap, someone is laughing and running away. I see a jay – a flash of brilliant blue feather against dusky pink, such strange exotic colours for an English woodland bird. A magpie squawks high up in the trees; it seems to be mocking me.

I have cramp now from kneeling hunched up for so long, but there are no sounds. Has everyone else gone? I uncurl myself, look round cautiously. It's said sometimes an old tramp lives in the woods, is he here now watching me? Should I call out?

I can see the sun on the fields beyond the wood. It looks warm there and I'm cold and shivering. I pick up my jam jar and run along the track to the stile, panting, breathing fast, terrified of being alone with all those branches like arms and fingers stretching out to scratch me, catch me.

I see a patch of red in the field.

Nettles sting my shins, I catch my hand on barbed

wire edging the wood, but I daren't call out or something might get me.

I climb the stile. It's sunny in the field; the others are by the pond looking for tadpoles. How could they have left me there, finished the game and gone without me? I won't cry. I wipe my muddy hand across my face, jump off the stile and walk nonchalantly, as Just William would have done, across the field and join the search for frogspawn.

My sister looks up as I splash into the water; she reaches out a hand to help me across the marshy bit but I won't take it. I go deeper into the water, which is cold on my boots; it swirls in patterns and light glints on the ripples. Behind the rushes I see a clump of frogspawn, swept out of the current and caught by the water weeds and rushes. I bend down and scoop some up in my jam jar. There's a squelching sound as it's detached from the rest of the jelly and it slimes over my fingers and is trapped in the glass. I pull off some pieces of weed to make the jar look less bare, then wade back to the shoreline of the pond.

We all have something in our jars. One of the boys has a minnow, there's a water snail too and the pond water is murky and full of strange sediments.

'Race you home,' shouts Ian. We know he'll win.

The sun is going down and shadows lengthening.

In the Easter Holidays, one objective was swimming lessons. We have to go by bus to Southsea, so with all our bags and baggage we clamber aboard, Anthea, Mum and me; we have front seats upstairs, a panoramic view down through the village, over Portsdown Hill, through the grinding streets of North End to the public swimming baths near the Guildhall in Portsmouth. As we go through the swing doors the damp atmosphere hits us, an aqua-green haze; the smell of the swimming baths laden with chlorine fills me with apprehension. There are bright white lights and the place is boomy and echoey. We squash into changing rooms the size of cupboards, the floor awash with water which runs down channels like Roman baths. We have ruched elasticated swimming costumes which tie at the neck and rubber swimming caps with chinstraps into which all our hair has to be twisted. We tiptoe along the side of the pool, sit cowering on the edge and then slip into the greeny-blue water.

The swimming instructor shouts at us as if we are dogs.

'Paddle, paddle, paddle with your feet, paddle harder!'

The instruction is harsh and unrelenting. I gulp mouthfuls of chlorinated water, my eyes sting, I splash with my legs, harder and harder, kicking and kicking and kicking. At last the teacher lets us draw breath and shows us a strange contraption intended to help us. It's like a large fishing hook, the size to catch a whale, and suspended from it is a rope and canvas life belt. We are slung into this and lowered down further and further until the belt hits the water and is gradually removed, and wriggling like tadpoles, we either sink or swim.

The first few times we sink like stones, humiliation, mouthfuls of water, despair, but slowly, slowly we learn to co-ordinate arms and legs, keep our heads up, kick and kick and kick until we can swim a width of the pool.

Exhausted, we crawl out covered with goose pimples, our hair like Medusa, teeth chattering. We peel off our swimming costumes and dried on rough towels, smelling of chlorine, we set off on the long journey home.

XIII

And then it's summer, warm, delightful summer.

It's a sunny morning and we're up early; we're always up early when the world is new. Pa comes in from the garden where he's been watering his seedlings and lettuces, cabbages and beans.

'Get your swimming togs,' he laughs.

Now it's a special morning, sunny and full of fun and an expedition with Pa.

'Where are we going?'

'Hayling Island,' he smiles. 'We'll be back for breakfast.'

So when we have found our scratchy beach towels, our ruched swimming costumes, mine blue with zebras on and Anthea's red with the same bizarre pattern, open toe sandals which are old and floppy and soft from last summer, we climb into the car. A black Ford Prefect has replaced the old khaki Ford Anglia. Pa revs the engine, hoots the horn and off we go, scrunching up the gravel drive. Mum closes the gate and we are off.

There are no cars on the roads, it's too early. We snake through the village under a blue June sky, sun beating down already, and Pa sings hymns, *Praise my Soul the King of Heaven*, and old army songs. We drive through Havant, past the church and the corn merchant, then we turn right to the narrow road bridge which takes us across the estuary to Hayling Island and the sea.

We can see it glittering in the morning light. Pa parks the car on the sand and we fall out and tumble across the dunes. We scramble into swimming costumes, helping each other and fumbling in our hurry, the sand grazes our feet and having piled our clothes in a heap we run down the beach.

Pa is already splashing in the water and gliding along with his favourite side stroke. The shoreline is deserted, but there's a rowing boat pushing out through the water with a couple of fishermen lapping the oars.

I want to go in the sea, but I'm not that good at swimming yet and the stones are cutting into my feet. I slow down, pick my way among the shells, mermaids' boats and pebbles and mud. Pa is far out now, scything slowly through the waves… what if he doesn't come back

– if the tide carries him away?

My sister is in and swimming, I have to do this too and not be the scaredy cat I so often feel, so I let the tide run over my toes, my shins, my knees up to my waist. It's freezing. I gasp.

Anthea is standing next to me splashing water on my head. 'Come on,' she says.

I sink my shoulders down, stretch out my arms and with a tug she pulls me off my feet. I waggle my toes like a tadpole's tail and kick harder, pull out with my arms and I'm swimming, just a few strokes but I can do it!

We play about in the waves, run up and down in the ripples. The tide is coming in now, the shore diminishing, we're still in the sea but closer to the dunes.

'Come on, show Pa you can swim!' shouts my sister.

And I imagine I'm a deep-sea diver. I hold my nose, plunge forward, and as I come up for air I see him swimming towards us on his back, hands clapping in the air.

We all splash about a bit more, then shake ourselves like dogs and run shivering up the beach to rescue our clothes before the sea swallows them. We struggle into Aertex shirts and shorts, sticky from salt water and not very dry. We're covered in goose pimples. Our hair is plastered against our heads, and when I lick the strands they taste of salt. We pull on sweaters, pick up our sandals and run for the car.

Pa is very jovial; he's loved our early morning adventure. He unlocks the door of the Prefect and we climb onto the back seats, warm with the sun, with the familiar and comforting smell of Pa's St Bruno flake tobacco. He sings again as we drive home and we see Puffing Billy, the steam train, shunting across the old wooden bridge, its struts lapped by the incoming tide, back to the mainland.

Back home it's only half-past eight, all the day still to unfold. Mum, looking calm and serene as always, in a summer dress with a pattern of peonies on it, has made us bacon sandwiches for breakfast.

XIV

My grandmother was about eighty when I was born. She looked ancient. She was small, bird-like in stature, with bright eyes in a face as wrinkled as an old map. Her thin grey hair was long and she plaited it and then twisted it into a bun at the nape of her tortoise neck She always wore black clothes, as if forever in mourning, and when she went out anywhere, even to walk along the road, she wore a small black hat with a veil, as if she was looking out from a fishing net and we were the sprats she had caught. And the worst thing of all, round her neck she wore a fur with the head of a dead pine marten, its teeth snarling and beady eyes staring as if it might leap off and attack us at any moment. She was Victorian and made no allowances for children or the twentieth century.

The house was dark and sombre, full of relics of my grandfather's naval voyages, tiger skin rugs which snarled down from the top of the stairs, the Benares tray from India engraved with intricate patterns glinting in the shadows, the three monkeys on the mantelpiece, Hear no Evil, See no Evil, Think no Evil, which seemed very inappropriate in that dark house filled with books.

We made ourselves as inconspicuous as possible and spent most of the visit in a garden overshadowed by tall, forbidding conifers. Sometimes we took our bikes and rode round and round the lawns; sometimes we played where the old Anderson shelter had been. We hopscotched on the drive and had games of French cricket under the apple trees. Pa spent most of the visit in the garden too, pruning the roses and fruit trees. He looked after her flowers, which she liked but he didn't (and never grew at home), zinnias set by the right in formal beds, gladioli in knicker elastic pink and antirrhinums, which in that garden seemed really to snap like snapdragons. We were given digestive biscuits and a glass of Rose's Lime Juice to drink on the back door step, but we dreaded having to go inside. All the rooms were dark but the bathroom was worst of all, with an Ascot heater which roared and rumbled and exploded like a volcano just when you were on the toilet and a high cistern which had a long chain, hard to reach but which, when pulled, unleashed the Niagara falls into the bathroom.

My grandmother lived with an enormous aunt, called Aziel, who hummed all day, towered over us, talked down to us, reduced us to helpless giggles but gave us very generous presents for our birthdays and at Christmas.

My grandmother tried to be kind.

Each time we visited her, just before we went home, she would say, 'Give me your hand.' Then with skeletal, talon-like fingers she would press a silver sixpence into our palms, screwing the coin down into our skin; we couldn't flinch because she grasped our hands so tightly. We had to look her in the eye and endure the ordeal. And say 'thank you.'

I'd rather not have had the money and escaped the torture.

XV

School filled lots of our lives, but the summer holidays were yawning spaces of time – hours and days to exist in. Then we lived the imaginary life we'd read about in books, of ponies and expeditions and camps in the orchard. The smell of privet flowers in the hedge would lure us down among the trees and we could climb into a world that was ours and hidden from the house.

We pitched a tent which Pa had bought from an army surplus shop, dragged out our sleeping bags and groundsheets, fixed up stick contraptions to hold bowls and cooking equipment and made spaces against the hedge as stables for our horses.

Mum gave us money to buy provisions. We got our bikes, pushed them up the gravel drive and set off to the shops. We crossed the road by the bus stop and then pedalled up the side roads through the estate of houses to a row of shops round the village green; grocer, baker, hairdresser, butcher and newsagent.

The bike ride there always seemed quite flat and easy, over tarmac roads devoid of traffic, past houses where women were housekeeping and dusting while their husbands were 'at the office'. We parked our bikes by the green and went into the dark grocer's shop. We bought baked beans and eggs and biscuits and butter, then to the butcher for sausages and bacon, and if we had money left we bought Mars bars or Kit Kats or Smarties and a Beano from the newsagent. Then, putting the shopping in baskets strapped to the handlebars of our bikes, we set off for home. We almost always went home by a different route, buoyed up perhaps by our purchases. With the thought of cooking our lunch on the campfire when we got back, we went via Chestnut Drive.

Had there been chestnut trees there once? If there had been they were all felled now.

Chestnut Drive sounds quite tame and suburban, but the road stretched further round the edge of the estate towards the woods and we puffed up a long, steep hill and from the top we could see across the village down to the main road and all the gardens and the church, marshes and sea in the distance. We could also see the dramatic switchback of the road home, swooping downhill and bending round in a wide arc. Probably the incline was insignificant, but to my seven-year-old self it was daunting.

'Ready?' Anthea asked me. And she set off, her plaits flying behind her, down the hill, round the bend until she was out of sight.

Now it's my turn, the houses along Chestnut Drive all seem deserted. There is never anyone walking along the pavement; it feels like no man's land. It's like being at the top of the diving board and knowing you have to jump, a gravelly feeling at the back of your throat and snakes wriggling in your tummy.

I take one foot off the ground, put it on the pedal, tighten my grip on the handlebars, and palms sweating, knees quaking, I push off.

The brakes on my bike aren't the best, the wind rushes past my face, the wheels are turning faster and faster and faster, so fast I can't see anything clearly any more, everything is blurred. I steer round the great curve, but I'm going too fast, the brakes won't hold, I'll crash... I see my sister waiting at the bottom of the hill, here's the garden with big blowsy begonias and gladioli, and then scarlet salvias and blue lobelia come into focus; I steer onto the verge, scuff my foot along the ground, my bike bumps over the grass, I hold my balance and stop.

We've done it again, defied the devil and all his works. We're safe.

'Come on slowcoach, are you ok?'

There's no answer other than 'Yes.'

Back on the old lane we bike more slowly back to the house.

Mum's waiting for us with home made lemon cordial; she's probably as relieved to see us back as we are to be home. We throw our bikes down on the grass and run down the garden path with our provisions. Mum has given us old pans, so we get dry grass and kindling and light the camp fire in the orchard and start cooking. It all smells good but it takes a long time.

Grasshoppers flit through the long grass and bees are murmuring in the privet flowers. We spent days and days playing in different parts of the garden all through the long weeks away from school.

And then, in soft September, from the safety of home, we went on holidays to Somerset and Devon, the other significant places in our lives.

XVI

We usually went on holiday at the season's turning, when the Kingston Black cider apples were ready for pressing, the last sweet peas were scrambling up the hazel sticks and twittering swallows gathered in the skies.

We set off in Pa's khaki-coloured Ford Popular, registration number ABK 141, on what felt like a momentous journey. We knew it would take a long time but the concept was elusive. It was so long that we had to take a picnic breakfast and picnic lunch, packed up in baskets the night before we left, ready on the kitchen table to pack into the car on the morning of departure.

We leave early to 'beat the traffic,' so early it seems it is only just light. Pa wears flannel trousers and a check shirt rather than his normal workday suits, and a corduroy cap instead of his hat. Mum is in a crisp cotton dress and we're in Aertex shirts and shorts; the leather sticks to the backs of our legs as we squirm about on the back seat of the car.

Gradually we drive out beyond the village, past the prefabs on Portsdown Hill, up beyond the fort at Southwick until we are beyond familiar territory and in a foreign land. We pass thatched cottages and isolated farms, fields of corn and fields of stubble, fields where cows graze among trees.

I'm excited, but I hate the smell of petrol and the airlessness of the car makes me feel sick. I keep my mouth shut, hoping that will help, and look out of the window at fields passing, snakes wriggling in my tummy all the while.

'We're making good time,' says Pa looking at his watch. 'Let's stop for breakfast.'

We all look out for a place to stop, a gateway into a likely field, not stubble because that's too scratchy to sit on, not one with cows in, not in the shade, not ploughed... until, like Goldilocks and the chairs, we find one that's just right. Pa swings the car off the road, the doors are opened and we fall out onto the grass verge.

Mum unloads the breakfast basket, and Pa spreads the travelling rug, an old plaid blanket of many summers. There are hard-boiled eggs, bread rolls, apples, biscuits, orange squash and a thermos of tea – it's like Rat and

Mole's picnic in *The Wind in the Willows* – and having eaten we race around, gulping in fresh air to brace ourselves for the next stage of the journey.

We wend our way through Dorset, a land of small farms where cattle graze in rich pasture, orchards are heavy with fruit, fields stand thick with corn, and then we wind up the long hill to Windwhistle Gap, eerie and menacing in winter but on a summer day the world is spread out before us, cloud shadows race over the hills and the wind sighs in the beech branches. Another stop in a field on top of the world, the lunch basket unpacked and the treat this time is Dairylea cheese triangles, wrapped in silver foil, packed in a round box, cheese and celery, cheese and ham, cheese and tomato, cheese and onion and 'just' cheese. We peel back the foil and squash the cheese triangles into bread rolls and run round the field eating them and getting hiccups and giggling with freedom. There are cream crackers, Cornish wafers, digestive biscuits, fruit cake and apples. We race around until we are almost dizzy and the sky is spinning.

Then it's back into the car for the last leg of the journey to the farm.

XVII

It's almost teatime when we drive through Merriott, a small village near Beadon Farm in Somerset. We turn up the lane, past the milk churn stand, over the bumpy track past the duck pond, and at last we have arrived.

Mrs Marks is there to greet us, hurrying out into the yard that smells of mayweed and cow dung, rubbing her hands on her floury apron. She looks the same as in my last year's long ago memories as I gaze out of the car window to wave to her.

She opens the car door. My legs have been sticking to the leather seats and I've felt all squashed up for the journey, as though I've been holding my breath because if I breathe I might be sick, or the dream might change; but now it's true, we are here.

'Hello my dears, and how was the traffic? You made very good time – I just looked at the clock and thought you'd be here soon and here you are! Well, isn't that lovely to see you all again, I'm just making tea. Come along in, come along in.'

I look up shyly at Mrs Marks. She is old, her face lined like a map with lots of contours. She has grey hair which is fixed in a loose bun with lots of wispy bits across her face. She has pale blue eyes and a kind smile. She takes my hand.

'My, how you've grown since last year! Come along duck, come inside and see Mr Marks, we're all in the kitchen.'

Her hand is warm and dry and wrinkled; mine is a bit sweaty after the journey. She leads us into the dark hall with a cool flagstone floor and round into the kitchen, where Mr Marks is sitting in his chair by the fire.

'Look who just arrived, flown back like the house martins here every summer. Look Henry, just look how these girls have grown!'

I'm wary of Henry Marks. He has a kind face, Mum and Pa like him and he talks to Pa about farming, but he never says much to us and we try to keep out of his way. He's very disabled; he can't move easily by himself and he sits by the fire even in high summer with his crutches beside him. He reminds me of the man who sells newspapers outside the Post Office at home, who stands on one leg; the other trouser leg is empty and pinned up where his knee should be and he calls out in a strange voice. His face is disfigured, and he sometimes haunts my dreams.

Henry Marks looks out from beneath beetle black eyebrows, then smiles and holds out his hand to greet us. I know I must shake it so I step forward.

When that is done, formalities over, we can dodge round the grown-ups and run about the garden and orchards. I can forget the strange apparatus in the bathroom and those frightening crutches until later. For now, we are free as birds flying up the garden, past lettuces and bean poles, up the cinder path past the barn and into the field.

We see Clappy, the old pony, and hear the hens clucking round the hen house. We go and look over the gate at the cows in the pasture and hear Mrs Marks calling us for tea; like chickens, we scuttle back to the house.

It's dark inside the farmhouse, and I blink after the sun outside; it's cool and smells, I think, rather exotic, not like home. I later learn that the smell which seems foreign and thrilling to me is in fact just damp, damp walls and floors and buildings crafted long ago of wood and lath and plaster and old stones.

Later, when it's bedtime and the bats are flying, we go up stairs which creak like branches in a gale, along the landing to our bedroom. It has a small window at one end, like an attic with low, sloping ceilings and lots of spiders and beetles. Bare floorboards are partially covered with a rag rug. There are two iron bedsteads, cool white sheets and pillows and jewelled crochet blankets with black edges and brilliant coloured squares like stained glass windows. On a little cupboard between the beds is a lamp and our night-time glasses of Kia Ora orange squash and two digestive biscuits. Mum has unpacked our pyjamas and Binky and my sister's dog and our books.

Now we have to go to the bathroom – swallows nest outside the window and dip and swoop and fly – but inside it looks like a torture chamber. There are metal frames around the toilet and a strange apparatus by the bath and basin; it reminds me of the dentist's surgery, full of shiny metal levers and gadgets, and I think if I touch them my fingers might be trapped. The light from a bare bulb casts shadows across the black and white tiled floor, across the basin and bath and there's a smell of medicines and carbolic soap. I don't like being in there by myself; the taps make gurgling noises, the cistern hisses and the chain from the toilet rattles slightly. I scurry through washing and cleaning my teeth and out of the door across the landing, then jump into bed and slide between cool, white sheets.

We never talked about it, the torture chamber bathroom. It's only now I realise all the equipment was for Henry Marks with his broken back. He had plummeted off a hayrick when he was younger. No one had thought he would survive, but he recovered and lived with the consequences.

We always get up early, at home and on holiday, and after breakfast we pull on boots and we're free to roam.

We wander across the yard with its elusive scent of mayweed, slosh through the cowshed where the cows have been milked and through to the dairy where milk is being poured from buckets into churns; it froths and splatters our boots and makes a musical, echoey sound as it gurgles up the metal sides of the churn. Lids are screwed on and the churns are heaved onto the cart to take them down the lane to be collected by the milk lorry. If we help pull the cart down the lane we're rewarded with a ride back.

Back at the farm we go to look at Clappy, the pony,

in the orchard, see the chickens in the barn, help to feed the pigs and collect duck eggs from the coop by the pond, it's slimy and muddy there. We ride on the Massey Ferguson tractor and watch the bales being put on the elevator to trundle to the top of the haystack.

In late September it's cider making time and after raking up all the apples from the orchard the buckets are taken to the cider house and an apple cake is made. All the apples are tipped into a trough layered with straw and Clappy is attached to a wheel; he circles round and round until all the juice is pressed and put into wooden kegs to ferment. We lead Clappy back to the field and make a great fuss of him, loving his dark eyes looking out from under his forelock and his soft, velvety muzzle. He puts up with the fuss for a while, lets us ride him bareback round the field, then shakes his mane and trots off to graze.

It's market day in Crewkerne, and everyone is about early. The kitchen table is covered with trays of eggs, pats of butter, cheese, onions, marrows, pots of geraniums, and we carry all these out to Mrs Marks' van. There are buckets of flowers too (I like these best), sweet peas, cornflowers, marigolds, snapdragons, larkspur, all the jewel colours with the dew still on them, picked by Mrs Marks when the sun was just up.

She pokes a pin into her hat, which is of soft straw with a ribbon round the brim, brushes her hands down her dress, glances round the kitchen to make sure nothing is forgotten, scoops up the black money tin which looks like a little treasure box, touches Henry gently on the shoulder and off she goes. Her van is an old grey Morris Minor, all the produce is in the back and we're wedged in between potatoes and marrows. She crunches the gears and we bump off up the lane.

'Here we are my dears, and there's your dad, already setting up the stall. That's a good dad you've got, girls.'

It's busy in the market, straw bales, wooden tables, chickens, calves, sheep. Mrs Marks lets down the back of the van so we can unload; she gives us plums, potatoes and carrots to carry to the stall.

She spreads out a big checked cloth and arranges all her goods. Last come the buckets of flowers, which she stands in the shade. I want the flowers to sell to make money for Mrs Marks, but secretly half hope they are left so we can take the blue-as-the-sky cornflowers back to the farm again.

All is ready, and Mrs Marks touches her hat into place

and settles down to serious selling.

'How much them duck eggs?' says a woman.

'They're fresh laid they are, lovely for cakes, my best ducks the Aylesburys laid them only yesterday. You'll win prizes if you make cakes for the show with them eggs, Mabel.'

Mabel smiles. 'All right then, I'll have half a dozen, and I'll have a bunch of them bright marigolds and a marrow for me marrow and ginger jam. How's Henry these days, Kate? A wonder ain't it that he's still alive – but he leaves you with plenty of work to do.'

'Well, it do keep me on my toes but he does what he can and I have good friends and my son comes when he can to help me out...'

'Terrible accident that were, terrible. Makes me blood run cold just to think of it and all those weeks in hospital when you didn't know whether he'd make it... you're a good woman, Kate Marks, and that's no mistake.'

'Well, enjoy the eggs Mabel, there's your change....'

And Mabel, large and like a ship in full sail, moves on round the market.

Mum takes us round the market too – the bread stall with cottage loaves and currant buns, the butcher with sausages and pigs' heads dripping blood, the seed merchant with sacks of grain and dog biscuits, chickens in coops with cheeping, chirping chicks, bantams with feathered legs looking like exotic Abyssinians and the raucous cockerel with flame-coloured feathers, just like my jigsaw at home.

We gaze for ages at the sweet stall, so many jars of temptation, flying saucers, clove balls, chocolate flakes......we pass calves, black and white Friesians, brown splattered Ayrshires and one lovely doe-eyed Jersey, her coat the colour of caramel and honeycomb.

The sun is high in the sky and the church clock strikes twelve when we go back to 'our' stall; Pa is packing up empty crates and putting them in the van.

'Did it go well?' asks Mum.

'You feel the weight of that my dear,' says Kate lifting the cash box. She was happy, the market had been worthwhile. The flower buckets were empty.

I knew when spring was come, not by the murmurous hum
Of bees in the willow trees,
But because there were cups and tops in the window
at Mrs Mopp's.

It's mid- afternoon, we're walking down the lane and our

shadows are stretching behind us. Pa is helping on the farm, he loves moving bales of hay and straw, so Mum has promised us a visit to the village shop. I keep putting my hand in my pocket to check my pocket money is still there, and jingling it with my fingers.

The bell jangles on the door as we push it open and the shop smells musty, of cooked cabbage and stew. Mum chats to Mrs Mopp while Anthea and I look among the tins of biscuits, bags of flour, cans of paraffin, toothpaste and shoe polish. In a corner by the window there are a few toys, comics, packs of cards, a doll, tin whistles, drawing pads, paints; and then I see a small green rubber hot water bottle in the shape of a cat, it has black eyes, stringy whiskers, tabby stripes, paws and in between its pointed ears the stopper where the water goes. I lift it out and clutch it, hoping I have enough money, and tug Mum's skirt to show what I've chosen. She smiles consent and says I have enough money for a quarter of flying saucer sweets and a postcard for Granny. Mrs Mopp beams, weighs out the sweets on the scale and tips them into a small paper bag.

'See you again next year m'dears,' she says as we hand over our money, and the door clangs behind us.

We walk back to the farm in the late afternoon sun,

past the churn stand, round the pond where the ducks are swimming, past the orchard and back through the garden where Mrs Marks is cutting sweet peas and the scent drifts on the air. Back to tea.

We usually ate in the kitchen at the farm, swallows swooping past the windows and Tessie and the cats lying by the fire. It was good, plain food, boiled eggs and apple pies but one day a neighbour had been invited to tea; she was rather grand and we had to eat in the dining room.

Mum has brushed my hair and put ribbons on my sister's plaits; I have to put on a skirt which has a farm print on it, pigs and sheep and cows and cornfields, and I feel a bit uncomfortable in white socks and sandals with very clean hands and face. We've had to keep out of the way for most of the day while preparations are made for the visitor.

The dining room is a sanctum we rarely enter. Heavy lace curtains hang over the windows, there are old family portraits and photographs on the walls, the chairs are covered in scratchy material which tickles the backs of my legs and the air in the room is heavy, as though it's been there a long time and is trying to escape.

There's a knock at the front door of the farmhouse,

which no one ever uses. I hide behind Mum's skirt as the door opens and Mrs Rice, the neighbour, steps in. She looks like someone from a circus or a pantomime, a cross between the nuns from our convent school and a clown, heavy with make-up. She is dressed in black lace with rows of pearls round her wrinkled neck, jewelled rings on her fat fingers and heavy, jangly bracelets round her wrist. She is large and loud and speaks in a strange voice which my sister says knowledgeably is a 'foreign accent'.

Mrs Marks is very welcoming. We hover behind feeling overawed. Mr Marks leans on his sticks, Pa stands back as always, Mum, in a pretty dress, conveys through the way she holds my hand that I must be well-behaved and my sister looks as though she's reading a book in her head. The neighbour, Mrs Rice (although I wonder now if it was spelt Reiss?) is ushered first into the dining room and when we follow, we can hardly believe our eyes. The table is covered with a cream lace cloth and is laden with food. Places are laid with the very best china, plates with gold rims which catch the light and little bone-handled knives and delicate cups and saucers.

Is this all for Mrs Rice? Who is she?

We wriggle into our seats, Mum listens as Mrs Rice gushes and laughs and beams at us all and Mrs Marks pours tea.

We eat wafer-thin bread and butter, crustless cucumber sandwiches, fruit cake with huge glacé cherries, sponge cake filled with lemon curd and sprinkled with icing sugar, ginger snap biscuits, shortbread, scones, and all the time Mrs Rice talks and laughs and holds court.

The relations in their portraits stare down at us, and I try not to drop my scone on the floor. Pa chats to Mr Marks about the harvest, Mrs Marks goes on pouring tea, Mum smiles and listens and Anthea and I swing our legs under the table until, at last, we're allowed to escape to the farmyard.

Mrs Rice left with all her pearls and folds of fat and wrinkles. We never saw her again.

And we too leave, with the swallows, home to our garden and school and everyday lives.

XVIII

It's slipping down the narrow track from the lane to the combe I remember first, sometimes in spring when the mossy stones were starred with primroses, once in winter when the world was white and snow drifted in banks along the hedge edges, most often in summer, down through a tunnel of green, ferns in the moss, honeysuckle clambering the banks, down through long shadows of trees to the bottom of the valley and the farm, White Oxen, bathed in sunlight and the world standing still.

We've all longed for the journey to be over and suddenly it seems we're whooshing through Devon, towards Totnes, towards Rattery, to South Brent and at last the farm.

White Oxen is a long, low, whitewashed stone building, the garden defended from the encroaching moor by stone walls, an orchard to one side. The house was built in Elizabethan times and added to by generations. Behind the house a stream plashed ceaselessly, fresh water running down from the moor for man and beast alike, and it's cool there on the north side, for the front of the house faces south, garnering all the light and warmth of every day. On the west side is a conservatory, smelling of geraniums and drying onions, full of cobwebs and spiders and ancient dust; on the east side, the dairy, dark and cool for cheese and butter making, fed with water from the stream and smelling of milk and cream. Up the slope behind the house are the farmyard and farm buildings – our summer haven.

Uncle Frank Pidgeon, who owned the farm, was a tall, strong, Devon farmer, the farm had been in his family for generations with its Red Devon cattle, pigs, chickens and a Massey Ferguson tractor replacing the farm horses.

He had been a bachelor for many years, but in his fifties he had met Jean Armstrong, a local teacher who had been our mum's best friend when they were at Whalley Range High School in Manchester together. It seemed even to us children a strange union, she a little pouter pigeon of a woman, only child of rich elderly parents, like a peacock in her finery and jewels and hats.

She never did a farming task in all her days; she didn't even touch the eggs until they had been washed and set in boxes on the stone slabs in the dairy.

Frank, whose head had been turned by this strange bird of paradise among the moorland sparrows, did everything on the farm, all the cooking and looking after the house and home. He cooked huge vegetable pies, roasted chickens and sides of beef, fried eggs and bacon and sausages and magicked cows' milk into cream and butter and cheese. He cleared muck from the yard, did the hedging and ditching as the year turned and seemed almost part of the land itself, the wild edges of Dartmoor.

It's early morning, the sun is shining through my bedroom window and shafts of light fall in patterns on the floor; as the curtains ripple in the breeze the patterns change and merge and divide like a kaleidoscope. I can hear swallows flittering in the eaves and the stream splashing on the stones behind the house. The sheets feel cool and I like the eiderdown on my bed, pale green with swirly Paisley patterns on it and smelling faintly of mothballs.

I don't like being in bed when it's light outside so I get up and look out of the window across the orchard. The grass is long and apples ripen on the trees.

Anthea's awake too, so we dress quietly and go downstairs through the stone-flagged hall to the boot room. We put on boots, unlatch the door, trail our fingers in the icy stream, splash water on our faces and wander into the yard in the sun. The farm cats sidle round our legs, soft fur tickling the backs of my knees and I kneel to stroke the marmalade one, who rolls on her back in the dust and swats the air with her paws.

Then up the slate steps to the granary, and our boots, wet from the stream, leave footprints on the stones. I push open the door and see dust motes in the beams of sunlight. The chickens, plump brown birds, are already clucking and burbling about in the straw. They strut towards us, sensing the pellets we have brought in the chicken scoop and they peck, peck, peck as I tip the scoop to let the pellets fall like rain. I bury my hands in straw to collect the eggs from the nesting boxes, warm, brown, speckled eggs which we carry down to the kitchen.

After breakfast we run off through the farmyard to the fields beyond, small fields like those of all Devon farms then, thickly hedged until the hedges petered out to thorn bushes and the moor encroached, wild and bleak.

The track was a quagmire in winter, rutted like a

quarry in summer; wind-torn trees arched overhead, branches twisted in south-westerly gales which roared in from the Atlantic across the wild sweep of the moor. We run along with Larkie the collie shadowing us and climb over the gate to the cows.

Hedgerows are laced with cobwebs, rose hips glisten in the sun, the grass is wet with dew. As we walk towards the cattle they lift their heads and low as we approach, their udders heavy with milk, and following Granny, the oldest cow who has mothered many fine calves, the Red Devon cows amble towards the gate, where Frank waits to shepherd them down the track. We follow, watching the early mist rise from the valley as the sun warms the land.

They make stately progress, the cattle, down between the hedges, across the stone yard, into the cool darkness of the shippen. Hooves slip on the stones as they take their places in the stalls. It's dark and quiet in the shippen. I can hear the cows breathing, see the breath from their huge wet nostrils, hear the clink of metal as we fasten the chains round their necks and they turn their great heads to look at me. We know not to stand behind them, not to move quickly or surprise them but to move gently and quietly; Frank teaches us all this; he passes on his knowledge and we absorb it like trusting creatures. We bring pails of water to wash their udders, they stare at us and blink Cyclopean dark eyes, and go on chewing the cud.

Frank gets the milking stool, gives us a milking cap, stained brown from the cow's hide and smelling of a mixture of milk and shippen. He holds the cow's tail over her back and sets down the bucket.

Anthea balances forward on the stool, leans in and starts pulling the teats. No sound but the cow's breathing, and then the swoosh of milk against pail. When her hands begin to ache it's my turn. Granny is generally patient enough to put up with our fumbling, but she has been known to kick. She peers round at me and moves restlessly, but Frank quietens her. Flies buzz round our heads. I squat down on the stool, press my head into her toffee-coloured flank and pull and squeeze the teats until the milk is flowing again and the pail is full and frothing. We give her cattle cake when we have finished, I love its sweet, malty scent, and when milking is finished, the cows lumber out of the shippen, blinking in the light of the yard.

The milk is poured into churns and taken down to the dairy. Pa helps us wash down the shippen; we sweep it all out with huge brushes, flood it with water, and sweep again and again until it is cleaned to Frank's satisfaction and we too go out blinking into the sunlight.

We go to find Rosa, an old, dark brown Dartmoor pony with a long shaggy mane and tail and a rough coat. Frank used to ride her out on the moor to see after the sheep and she pulled the milk cart, but now she spends her days in the orchard. We offer her apples and she comes to meet us. We brush her mane, untangle her tail and curry-comb the mud from her flanks. We imagine we have other horses too and pretend we are riding across the moor on a mission for Gloriana when Drake was playing bowls on Plymouth Hoe. We are only in the orchard for the day, but the dreams are ours.

When Rosa has had enough of our game we go back to the barn. A wooden ladder leans up against the bales. The hay smells sweet of summer grass, bluebottles buzz against the dusty window, cobwebs stretch across the beams. We climb the ladder, hand over hand, rung after rung; I clench my teeth and force myself to the top. The ladder wobbles perilously as I step off onto the highest bales. I daren't look down, my head is spinning.

Anthea shouts, 'Go!'

Then, as if on a sledge in snow I slide pell mell down

the slope of straw. It's terrifying and exciting. Chickens flutter and squawk as I scramble up and shake the hay from my hair; it scratches the back of my neck and the dust makes me sneeze. Chickens go back to pecking grain and I climb the ladder again and again.

Sometimes we had expeditions. Picnics were packed in baskets and we drove across the moor to spend the day by streams, damming the flow of water with stones and redirecting its course; we saw the heather blaze and heard the air thick with bees; we walked miles to 'points of interest' which turned out to be not very interesting at all; we climbed Haytor rock and saw for miles across the county to the sea.

Once, when we were about to head back to the farm, a mist came rolling in from the sea and cloaked the moor. The fog distorted shapes and sounds; it clung to our hair and felt like cobwebs on our faces. We stumbled back across tracks towards where we had left the car by a stream, desperate to avoid bogs and marshes which, so legend had it, would suck you into their depths if you stepped into them. The mist grew thicker, ponies loomed out of the miasma, first you could hear their breathing and their hooves pawing the ground and then their shapes would appear, rather menacing and unfriendly, following us closely. Then the siren wailed from Princetown prison, rooks crashed in the trees, stones slopped in the ponds, the wailing continued; we all knew what the siren meant, a prisoner had escaped and was at large on the moor. I felt like Pip in *Great Expectations* trying to get out of the clutches of Magwitch. Would we reach the car before we were snatched, or worse?

We stumbled on, hoping we were going in the direction of the road and not walking in circles, disoriented by the fog which was cold now and muffled all sight and sound. We heard a clatter of hooves on tarmac; we must be by the road, we must be near the village. We hurried on and found the bridge over the stream and the road and the car.

The siren wailed again at night when we were back at White Oxen. Owls hooted. The doors were locked and barred and all the outbuildings bolted.

By morning the fog had lifted, sun streamed into the valley again. I don't know what happened to the prisoner.

Sometimes we went to the sea and swam in freezing water, teeth chattering, arms goose-pimpled, or went to Brixham to watch fishermen unloading their catch, or walked up along the cliffs at Berry Head looking far out to sea.

Once we went to Dartmouth, on a grey day when nothing quite sparkled. We had looked at boats and walked along the shore, been to the museum and skimmed stones in the waves. We were going back to the car when we saw a bookshop. We had some money, given as usual by Granny for our holiday and as yet unspent. The shop had bow windows and was dark and dusty inside, but there were shelves and shelves of books. Pa went to look at the history section, Mum to the poetry and plays and the bookshop owner, who was quite friendly, encouraged us to look round the children's section and showed us horse books and history books, travel books and school stories and then left us to our search. I found a book called *Now We are Six* by A.A. Milne, and having picked it out from the shelf and looked at the pictures and poems I held it tightly; I'd borrowed it from the library at home and really liked the poems. I went over to Mum and whispered that I had found what I wanted.

We went to the counter.

'What a lovely book you've chosen, do you have your money?' The bookshop owner was tall and thin and wore glasses. Her hair was scraped back into a bun.

I proffered a ten-shilling note and she pinged the cash register and gave me some change.

She chatted to Mum and then said, 'Would your daughter like the book signed by the author's son? Christopher Robin is coming in today and I can ask him to sign it for you.'

'That's so kind but we're just leaving, perhaps another....'

'Oh it's no trouble, I'm sure he'd love to do it. Wait a moment. I can see him coming, we'll ask him now.'

A tall, gangly man came into the shop, fair rumpled hair and an old tweed jacket. The bookshop owner explained. I felt rather embarrassed. My book was taken and Christopher Robin Milne found a fountain pen in his pocket and signed my book in tiny writing. Mum tugged my hand to remind me to say thank you. The bookshop owner beamed. Christopher Robin looked a bit disconcerted. He put his pen away and disappeared up the wooden stairs at the back of the shop.

The book is on my bookshelf in the kitchen, still.

Another time, one long, sunny afternoon, we went to Dartington Hall. I remember dark shadows of cypress trees across the lawn and buying *The Woolpack* by Cynthia Harnett, one of the early Puffin books. I read it over and over again.

Many afternoons we mooched about the farm. We

had catapults made from forked sticks and learnt to find robins' pincushions in the hedges, oak apples in the trees and fossils among the stones. We learnt to shoot with bows made from yew wood and tautened with string, arrows fashioned from hazel sticks and flighted with feathers. We became archers at the Battle of Crècy, fought the Sheriff of Nottingham or followed Hereward the Wake into the marshes.

There were grey days and wet days and cold days, but most of all there were days filled with September sunlight and shadows, and however the day unfolded we were always back at the farm for evening milking, shadows lengthening across the yard, and by the end of the holiday the swallows were gathering on the roofs of the barns, feasting on late flies before their long journey home.

We went sometimes in spring when the lanes were starred with primroses, and once in winter when snow covered the moor and the drive down to White Oxen was as icy as the Cresta run, but mostly we went in September and then left for our other world. The happenings and happiness of those days fuelled our lives.

We went back, year after year, like swallows.

www.ingramcontent.com/pod-product-compliance
Lightning Source LLC
Chambersburg PA
CBHW021638080526
44584CB00015BA/1449